MY FIRST
Mass Book

Catholic CLASSICS

Written
Sr. Karen Cavanaugh

Illustrated by
William Luberoff

Regina
Press

Artwork © Quadriga, NY 2005
Text © The Regina Press

My Mass Book

We go to Church on Sunday,
   to the beautiful house of God.

Like a mother and father calling
   their children,

God says: Come to my house.
Come with your brothers and sisters,
   your neighbors and friends.

All of You,
   Come to my house.

I want to show you my love
   and give you my gifts.
   Come to my house.

Jesus promised: "Where two or three
   meet in my name
   I shall be there
   with them."

Going Into God's House

Going into God's house,
    we meet other people there,

Some you know and some you don't,
    but God brings all of us there.

All of us belong to one family,
    God's family.

Look, the altar table is set,
    candles are burning to welcome us
    going into God's house.

Put your fingers into the holy water
    at the church door.

At your baptism God made you his child
    by water and God's word.

We belong here in God's house.

Gathering Together

Together we stand and welcome the priest,
　　He is like Jesus Christ who came
　　to gather us all.
And we welcome God's word in the
　　Holy Book,
　　God's word that will light up
　　our minds.
So we sing a song in our hearts,
　　and praise our God together.

*The priest makes the Sign of the Cross
　　to begin our prayer:*
　　In the Name of the Father,
　　and of the Son,
　　and of the Holy Spirit.
We answer: Amen.

The priest greets us: The Lord be with you.
We say: And also with you.

Being Sorry

Jesus came to show us
    how to love God and one another.

He came to take away sin
    and make us friends with everyone.

He came to open our eyes and hearts
    to see what is good in everything
    around us.

And so we say we are sorry
    for not loving God and one another,
    for not being friends with everyone,
    for not seeing how good everything is.

And God hears our prayer.
    Lord, have mercy.
    Christ, have mercy.
    Lord, have mercy.

We All Say: Glory to God

When Jesus was born the angels sang:
Glory to God in the highest,
and peace to his people on earth.

The night air filled with their song,
and heaven and earth rejoiced.

Glory to Jesus Christ, God's Son,
they sang, praising the Child,
the humble Lamb, who would die for
the sins of the world.

We too sing with the angels, Glory to God,
and peace to his people on earth.

We praise the Father, our heavenly King,
and Jesus Christ his only Son,
the Holy one,
the Lord,
and the Holy Spirit. Amen.

Listening to the Word of God

We listen as the bible is read.
All of its stories are old.
Some even go back to the beginning,
    when the earth and heavens
    were made.

When God put the stars in the sky and
    the sun to warm the flowering fields.
Some stories tell of Abraham whom God
    made the father of many nations.
Then there are stories of Moses who led
    the Jews out of Egypt,
And great prophets like Isaiah
    and Jeremiah, and apostles like
    Peter and Paul.
We remember how good God was to them,
    and realize how good God is to us.
So we say: Thanks be to God.

The Gospel

"The Lord be with you," *the priest or deacon says.*

"And also with you," *we answer.*

Then we sign our forehead, our lips and
our heart with a small cross.
Yes, the Lord is with us as we listen to
his gospel.
We open our minds, and our hearts
to the stories of Jesus.
And tell others these stories with our own
lips.
At Christmastime we hear stories of Jesus'
birth in Bethlehem, how the Wise Men
came to visit him, and how
he was baptized.
At Easter we hear stories of his death
and resurrection.

Through the year listen to the stories
of Jesus, how he cured sick people;
and cared for those who were poor,
and wept for those who were sad.

We Tell God
We Believe in Him

We believe in God the Father,
and in Jesus Christ, his only Son,
and in the Holy Spirit, the giver of life.

The stories we hear from the Bible,
and the words of the homily bring
a prayer of faith to our lips.

Yes, God made the heavens and the earth,
and God is our good Father.

We believe in Jesus Christ, who was born
of the Virgin Mary,
suffered under Pontius Pilate,
was crucified, died and was buried.

On the third day he rose again
and went up into heaven.

We believe in the Holy Spirit,
the Holy Catholic Church,
the forgiveness of sins,
and life everlasting. Amen.

We Pray for Everybody in the World

God is so good.

God loves us and wants good things
for us.

So we ask God to remember
- everybody in the world
- our pope, bishops and priests
- our family and friends
- the poor and the sick
- the lonely and the suffering
- and whatever we need ourselves.

We offer our prayer through Jesus Christ,
our Lord.
Amen.

We Present Our Gifts.

We bring gifts of bread and wine
    to the priest at the altar.
They have come a long way
    from the fields of the earth
    where bread was once grains of wheat
    and wine was grapes on the vine.
They have come a long way
    planted in the soil,
    warmed by the sun in the sky,
    nourished by the rain that falls and
    the air that is everywhere.
They have come a long way
    as human hands took these gifts of
    our earth and made bread and wine.
So we bring them to God, who gave them
    to us, and Jesus through these gifts
    will give Life to the world.
Blessed be God forever!

Our Prayer of Thanksgiving

On the night before he died,
when Jesus was at supper with his friends,
he took bread from the table and said:
Take this all of you, and eat it:
This is my Body which will be
given up for you.

Then he took a cup filled with wine,
thanking God, he gave it to his friends
and said:
Take this, all of you, and drink from it.
This is the cup of my Blood,
It will be shed for you and for all so
that sins may be forgiven.

Then he said to them:
Do this in memory of me.

We remember with joy,
all that Jesus did to save us.
Remember us, O Lord Jesus Christ.

We Pray as Jesus Taught Us

Our Father, who art in heaven,
    hallowed be thy name;
    thy kingdom come;
    thy will be done on earth
    as it is in heaven.

Give us this day our daily bread;
    and forgive us our trespasses
    as we forgive those
    who trespass against us;

and lead us not into temptation,
    but deliver us from evil.

For the kingdom, the power and the glory
    are yours, now and forever.

We Offer One Another a Sign of Peace

Jesus wanted his friends to live in peace
  together.
He always prayed they would love one
  another.

And so we turn to those who are near us,
  to our parents, brothers and sisters,
  to a stranger there beside us.

And we wish them peace:
  Peace be with you.
  We want to live together in this world as
  one family,
  in peace and unity.

We Receive Communion

*When the priest holds before us the
    Body of Christ,
    he says:* "This is the Lamb of God."

And we say: "Lord, I am not worthy to
                receive you
                but only say the word and
                I shall be healed."

In the Bread and Wine we receive the
    Body and Blood of Christ.
As we go to receive Communion,
    we receive Jesus Christ,
    and as we receive him we are,
    with everyone else, one body with him.
He will give us life, and truth,
    and strength.

*The priest or minister gives you the Host
    and says:*
    "The Body of Christ"

And you answer: "Amen."

We Leave God's House in Peace

We leave the church on Sunday,
　　the beautiful house of God,
　　to love and serve the Lord
　　everyday in every way.

"Go, in Peace," *says the priest,*
　　blessing us with the Sign of the Cross.
"Thanks be to God," *we answer,*
　　as we sign ourselves.

And we sing a song of praise.
　　Jesus will be with us,
　　within us, and before us.
　　Jesus will be beside us,
　　a friend at our side,
　　to guard us from danger
　　to lead us in peace.

The Catholic Church

On Sundays and holydays good Catholics go to a Catholic Church. All who attend hear the same message, the message Jesus left for all men when he lived on earth. The message tells us how to live here so that we may find our way back to his home in heaven.

The Church is far more than just buildings. The Church is made up of people, men, women and children whose world is marked with the sign of Baptism.

Even if all church buildings were destroyed, the Catholic Church would be still alive. It would live in the hearts of its people. We call the love and devotion people have in their hearts for God, the invisible Church on earth.